STILL CAN'T SAY GOODBYE:
Sudden losses makes it hard

By

Kiera George

Copywriting

All right reserved. No part of this publication may be reproduced, distributed or transmitted in any form or by any means, including photocopying, recording or other electronic or mechanical methods, without prior written permission of the publisher, except in the case of brief quotation embodied in critical reviews and certain non-commercial uses permitted by copyright law.
Copyright© Kiera George, 2022.

Table of contents

Chapter 1

You left without a word

Losing my father early on of seven, was certainly not a simple encounter. He passed on early on, I never realized he experienced diabetes, I just knew him as a solid, sure and a sweet visually impaired man. Still in grade school, playing with companions during break time, when my sibling's companion ran towards me and said there was a function at my home. I figured it very well may be a birthday celebration, so my siblings and I pursued home shutting time, just to see my father's image hung outside the house. Individuals strolling all through the house supporting my mother. She was completely nestled into the edge of the bed crying and she said my father died that morning. Still in shock, I cried as a youngster that I actually couldn't accept he kicked the bucket. His demise left a void nobody could fill. I can't remember my father being debilitated, he generally had a major grin all over, he was consistently a cheerful individual, continuously paying attention to his traditional music on Sundays, Congo music on Thursdays and paying attention to BBC news each and every day. His end was something I was unable to make sense of, it came as a shock and to that end my melancholy waited longer than I anticipated. On the 18 of July 2000, was a Tuesday I can't fail to remember in a rush.

Unexpected demise of a friend or family member can be so excruciating and wrecking. The shock and unexpected once-over of
feeling whenever you know that he/she isn't returning, is a particularly horrendous yet unavoidable inclination. By then, there are so many profound surge of recollections of the departed that continue to play in your mind.

Individuals who are influential for our lives can give us monstrous security and inspiration. At the point when these individuals pass on, it can make us feel lost and aimless, as well as profound agony and any pragmatic hardships because of the deprivation.

The aggravation where you never got the opportunity to bid farewell is a seriously horrendous inclination particularly when you have either an exceptionally impressive relationship with the departed or, you are not in a decent connection with the departed. For my situation, I had an exceptionally amazing connection with my father cause I was his most memorable girl. We had this extraordinary bond which I never had with my mother. My father was the nearest to me and he partakes in my thoughts and was consistently there to put me through, with such a cozy relationship as this, it is entirely reasonable that I can't move past the passing of my dad make I never got the opportunity said goodbye to him, I never had the opportunity to say a legitimate farewell, and it's difficult pushing ahead. I got to do things alone, in secondary school I saw understudies discussing their involvement in their fathers and I just tuned in without saying a word since I realized I had none to share. I assume I comprehend how one could wish to control the wild by holding demise close in a confidential space, aside from the conventional and the unavoidable inquiries that one can't respond to.

However, not sharing is its own type of mercilessness. By not permitting friends and family to set themselves up, to express farewell here and there, denies us of the endowment of extreme giving.

In any case, how is it that I could have realized he'd be gone before long? The truth we as a whole face is that we can't at any point be aware.

I was unable to find a genuine definition for 'sadness trigger' so I'm feeling free to characterize it for you. A misery trigger is anything that raises recollections connected with a misfortune. Triggers might be self-evident and simple to expect - like a birthday or an occasion - or they might be surprising - like spotting somebody who seems to be your cherished one in a group. A melancholy trigger could bind to a particular memory or feeling, or it very well might be something that blazes into cognizance and just leaves you with a feeling of bitterness and longing.

Despondency triggers are disturbing in light of the fact that they open the conduit for compulsory personal recollections. These are the recollections that jump into your head with practically no work on your part to review them. They could hit you out of the blue as you're driving down the road, sitting at your work area at work, or while you're microwaving popcorn. A considerable lot of these recollections are harmless, while others, particularly those related with expired friends and family, can leave you with a genuine scope of sentiments.

To explain, these recollections aren't completely irregular and don't really appear suddenly; typically, a sight, sound, tune, smell, word, or another memory triggers them. These recollections that are frequently connected areas of strength intrude on your mind's standard programming, and the interruption might be blissful cheerful euphoria delight, or it might cause you to feel like you've been hit in the stomach.

For those who've as of late lost a friend or family member, realizing these triggers are out there can cause a considerable measure of uneasiness. You could fear being walloped by tokens of your cherished one, their passing, and their nonattendance, particularly just after a misfortune when your feelings are crude and labile. A few mourners will answer by disposing of and staying away from updates like items, individuals and spots; others will attempt to fight their direction through, developing less and less humiliated by every public explosion of feeling.

Under a thick obscurity of profound disquietude in the main part of fall, it is consistently precarious for me to keep up with point of view. In any case, I battle the desire to keep away from updates in light of the fact that, in spite of the fact that they seem like the adversary during seasons of obscurity, my compulsory recollections are generally the specific inverse. It happens frequently enough that a tune, a spot, or a face helps me to remember something brilliant about my dad -

enough so I would get through any measure of
agony to recall the upside.

Chapter 2

Grief and depression

At the point when you lose a person or thing dear to you, feeling torment and grief is normal. The melancholy cycle is typical, and a great many people go through it. Be that as it may, when melancholy assumes control over your life and you start to feel miserable, defenseless, and useless, then now is the right time to converse with your PCP about differentiating between ordinary pain and sadness.

What Is Grief?
Pain is a characteristic reaction to death or misfortune. The lamenting system is a chance to properly grieve a misfortune and afterward mend. The cycle is helped when you recognize misery, track down help, and permit time for pain to work.

Every year, somewhere in the range of 5% and 9% of the populace loses a nearby relative.

However, that is by all accounts not the only sort of misfortune that can cause misery. Individuals can feel misfortune when:

- They become isolated from a friend or family member
- They lose an employment, position, or pay
- A pet bites the dust or takes off
- Kids venture out from home
- They have a significant change in life, for example, getting a separation, moving, or resigning.

While we as a whole vibe despondency and misfortune, and every one of us is remarkable in the ways we adapt to our feelings. Some individuals have solid adapting abilities. They're ready to feel sorrow without neglecting to focus on their everyday obligations.
Others don't have the adapting abilities or backing they need. That impedes the lamenting system.

How Would We Respond to Distress and Misfortune?

There are explicit phases of distress. They reflect normal responses individuals have as they attempt to get a handle on a misfortune. A significant piece of the mending system is feeling and tolerating the feelings that come because of the misfortune.

Individuals go through normal phases of sorrow. As per Kübler-Ross, the five phases of misery are:

- Denial
- Anger
- Bargaining
- Depression
- Acceptance

Denial, deadness, and shock: Deadness is a typical response to a demise or misfortune and ought to never be mistaken for "not mindful." This phase of pain shields us from encountering the power of misfortune. It tends to be valuable when we need to make some move, like arranging a burial service, telling family members, or exploring significant papers. As we travel through the experience and gradually recognize its effect, the underlying disavowal and skepticism blurs.

Bargaining: This phase of sadness might be set apart by steady contemplations about what "might have been finished" to forestall the passing or misfortune. Certain individuals become fixated on contemplating explicit ways things might have been done any other way to save the individual's life or forestall misfortune. On the off chance that this phase of melancholy isn't managed and settled, the individual might live with extraordinary sensations of responsibility or outrage that can disrupt the mending system.

Depression: In this stage, we start to understand and feel the genuine degree of death or misfortune. Normal indications of despondency in this stage incorporate difficulty resting, unfortunate hunger, exhaustion, absence of energy, and crying spells. We may likewise have self indulgence and feel forlorn, confined, vacant, lost, and restless.

Once in a while, a significant melancholy can create alongside the typical sensations of misfortune or misery connected with distress. Though ordinary trouble as a feature of a sorrow response might die down following a while, significant discouragement is a clinical problem that is not quite the same as expected pain, can happen whenever (even in the quick repercussions of a passing of misfortune), and expects treatment to be settled.

Anger: This stage is normal. It as a rule happens when we feel vulnerable and frail. Outrage can come from a sensation of surrender due to a passing or misfortune. In some cases we're angry at a higher power, at the specialists who really focused on a lost cherished one, or toward life overall.

Acceptance/Acknowledgment: In time, we can find a sense of peace with every one of the feelings and sentiments we encountered when the passing or misfortune occurred. Recuperating can start once the misfortune becomes incorporated into our arrangement of life encounters.

All through our lives, we might get back to a portion of the previous phases of despondency, like sadness or outrage. Since there are no standards or time cutoff to the lamenting system, everybody's recuperating interaction will be unique.

What Can Hinder the Recuperating System?
A few things can hinder or dial back the mending system following a passing or misfortune. They include:

- Staying away from feelings
- Enthusiastic ways of behaving
- Limiting sentiments
- Exhausting at work
- Abusing medications, liquor, or different substances as a method for managing profound uneasiness

What Things Could Assist with Settling Melancholy?

Permit a lot of chance to encounter contemplations and sentiments.

Trust in a confided face to face about the misfortune.

Express sentiments transparently or compose diary sections about them.

Find mourning gatherings in which there are others who've had comparable misfortunes.

Recollect that crying can give a delivery.

Look for proficient assistance assuming that sentiments are overpowering.

What can really be done on the off chance that My Anguish Will not Disappear?

On the off chance that distress proceeds and causes a delayed and profound sadness with actual side effects like unfortunate rest, loss of craving, weight reduction, and even considerations of self destruction, you might have a condition known as confounded mourning. Chat with your PCP straightaway.

Chapter 3

Years past and it still hurt

Many individuals consider distress a solitary example or as a brief time frame of torment or trouble in light of a misfortune - like the tears shed at a friend or family member's memorial service. Yet, lamenting incorporates the whole profound course of adapting to a misfortune, and it can keep going quite a while. The cycle includes a wide range of feelings, activities, and articulations, all of which assist an individual with grappling with the departure of a friend or family member.

We might hear the hour of melancholy being depicted as "would be expected lamenting," yet this essentially alludes to a cycle anybody might go through, and not even one of us encounters sadness the same way. This is on the grounds that sadness doesn't appear to be identical for everybody. Also, every misfortune is unique.

How long does the lamenting system endure?
Since every individual laments in an unexpected way, the length and power of the feelings individuals go through changes from one individual to another. Lamenting is excruciating, and the people who must have experienced a misfortune be permitted the time they need to communicate their distress.

In spite of the fact that sorrow is portrayed in stages or stages, it might feel more like a thrill ride, with high points and low points. This can cause it difficult for the dispossessed individual to feel any feeling of progress in managing the misfortune. An individual might feel much improved for some time, just to become miserable once more. Once in a while, individuals can't help thinking about how long the lamenting system will endure, and when they can anticipate some help. There's no solution to this inquiry, however a portion of the variables that influence the force and length of lamenting are:

- Your relationship with the individual who kicked the bucket
- The conditions of their passing
- Your own background

It's normal for the distress interaction to require a year or longer. A lamenting individual should determine the profound and life changes that accompany the passing of a friend or family member. The aggravation might turn out to be less extreme, yet it's not unexpected to feel sincerely engaged with the departed for a long time. In time, the individual ought to have the option to involve their close to home energy in alternate ways and to reinforce different connections.

For certain individuals, sensations of misfortune are incapacitating and don't further develop even after time elapses. This is known as muddled misery, now and again called tireless complex mourning problem. In convoluted misery, difficult feelings are so durable and extreme that you experience difficulty recuperating from the misfortune and continuing your own life.

Various individuals follow various ways through the lamenting experience. The request and timing of these stages might shift from one individual to another:

Acknowledging the situation of your misfortune
Permitting yourself to encounter the aggravation of your misfortune
Changing in accordance with another reality in which the departed is as of now not present
Having different connections
These distinctions are ordinary. Yet, on the off chance that you can't travel through these stages over a year after the demise of a friend or family member, you might have convoluted distress. Assuming this is the case, look for treatment. It can assist you with dealing with your misfortune and recover a feeling of acknowledgment and harmony.

Indeed, even with expected misfortunes, shock and skepticism are very common.However, unexpected passings don't permit the mourner to get ready for the misfortune, which makes it extraordinarily hard to try and start the lamenting process.With no opportunity to plan, shock and doubt pull you in, holding you back from venturing out to adapt to the misfortune.

In all honesty, I feel there is no measure of time expected to misery a friend or family member that far affects your physical and emotional well-being. Not a day goes by without the prospect of my father springing up, I wish he was as yet alive, yet it's been 22 years sooner or later it's as yet protected to express "years past it actually stings".

Chapter 4

Recovering from grief

I really want to let you know that, notwithstanding critical misfortune, we don't "recuperate" from grief.

Indeed, I'm utilizing the regal "we" since you and I are every one of the a piece of this club.I likewise need to let you know that not recuperating from despondency doesn't destine you to an existence of misery. Allow me to console you, there are a large number of individuals out there, at this moment, carrying on with ordinary and intentional lives while likewise encountering continuous sorrow.

Every one of the things you've caught wind of moving past despondency, returning to ordinary, and continuing on - they are deceptions of loving somebody who has passed on. Please accept my apologies, I know us human-individuals value things like conclusion and goal, yet this isn't the manner by which sorrow goes.

It is not necessarily the case that "recuperation" doesn't have a spot in despondency - it's just 'what' we're recuperating from that should be reclassified. To "recuperate" signifies to get back to a typical condition of wellbeing, brain, or strength, and as numerous

would validate, when somebody extremely critical passes on, we always avoid a pre-misfortune "typical". The misfortune, the individual who kicked the bucket, our pain - they all get coordinated into our day to day routines and they significantly change how we experience and experience the world.

What will, ideally, return to an overall pattern is the degree of serious inclination, stress, and misery that an individual encounters in the long stretches of time following their misfortune. So maybe we recuperate from the serious misery of sadness, however we don't recuperate from the actual despondency.

I for one think there are ways we adapt to despondency without it horrendously affecting the deprived. I still distress the deficiency of my father yet I harp generally on the beautiful recollections I had with him. Along these lines, there are ways which we adapt and they are expressed beneath.

1. Recollect and commend the existence of your adored one
Lamenting a friend or family member is a difficult and mixed insight since a piece of that sorrow cycle is reviewing recollections of the individual you have lost. A significant piece of recuperating is recollecting and discussing your cherished one.
Frequently the term festivity of life is utilized as an option in contrast to a burial service, as this expression offers a suggestive quality that praises the memory of the departed and celebrates what this individual brought to the world. By permitting yourself to recall, discuss and commend the existence of your friends and family, you can respect them in significant ways.

2. Acknowledge your feelings

Despondency can be such an excruciating encounter that occasionally individuals effectively keep away from their sentiments in the expectation of saving themselves the uneasiness. With regards to melancholy, evasion doesn't work. Keeping away from sorrow might seem like the best other option, however the agony looks for you, and in the long run, it should be confronted and experienced.

Feelings connecting with despondency can fluctuate enormously. You might discover that your sentiments change quickly and it is impeccably considered common. Recognize your sentiments, not exclusively to yourself however to other people. As you are lamenting, you might encounter bitterness, culpability, outrage and regret. It is additionally normal for liberating sensation to arise, especially if the cherished one had been anguish.

This scope of feelings is an ordinary piece of lamenting. Recognizing it and communicating it is a sound method for exploring the sadness cycle. As you discuss your sentiments and recollect the existence of your adored one, others are probably going to do likewise, which can assist with working with their recuperating as well as your own.

You can attempt to smother your misery, yet you can't keep away from it for eternity. To mend, you need to recognize the aggravation. Attempting to keep away from sensations of misery and misfortune just drags out the lamenting system. Unsettled misery can likewise prompt entanglements, for example, sadness, tension, substance misuse, and medical issues.

3. Deal with yourself
Despondency can be so extraordinary on occasion that it can slow down your capacity to see your own requirements. Distress and taking care of oneself is a significant thought. Despite the fact that it might feel irrelevant at the time, it is essential.

Dealing with yourself can be characterized in numerous ways and is really a singular encounter that no one but you can decide. What does taking care of oneself resemble for you? Getting satisfactory rest, taking care of actual wellbeing and remaining associated with companions are useful ways of keeping your health on target during seasons of misery.

Dealing with yourself might mean expressing no to additional obligations or commitments for some time. Misery can be debilitating and may imply that you really want to safeguard your energy until you begin to feel quite a bit improved. Taking care of yourself during seasons of pain is a fundamental concentration to push toward mending. It isn't egotistical, narcissistic or eager. Taking care of oneself is an approach to regarding your own wellbeing and health as you recuperate from a significant misfortune. Taking care of oneself is self-empathy.

Express your sentiments in a substantial or imaginative manner. Regardless of whether you're not ready to discuss your misfortune with others, it can assist with recording your contemplations and sentiments in a diary, for instance. Or on the other hand you could deliver your feelings by making a scrapbook or chipping in for a purpose connected with your misfortune.

Attempt to keep up with your leisure activities and interests. There's solace in daily schedule and returning to the exercises that give you pleasure and associate you nearer to others can assist you with finding a sense of peace with your misfortune and help the lamenting system.

Try not to allow anybody to let you know how to feel, and don't let yourself know how to feel all things considered. Your distress is your own, and no other person can let you know when now is the ideal time to "continue on" or "deal with it." Let yourself feel anything you feel without humiliation or judgment. It's alright to be irate, to shout at the sky, to cry or not to cry. It's likewise OK to giggle, to track down snapshots of euphoria, and to give up when you're prepared.

Care for your actual wellbeing. The psyche and body are associated. At the point when you feel great actually, you'll be better ready to sincerely adapt. Battle pressure and weariness by getting sufficient rest, eating right, and working out. Try not to utilize liquor or medications to misleadingly numb the agony of despondency or lift your temperament.

4. Contact others managing misfortune

One of the most incredible ways of strolling through your sadness and mend from by contacting others are managing misfortune. Helping other people manage despondency is a commonly valuable undertaking. It is a strong encounter to sit with other people who are going through similar feelings of sadness and misfortune. Bantering with other people who are lamenting offers a feeling of predictability that is rare during times of distress. The sensation of association with other people who are lamenting can offer expectation and mending to all included.

Not just contacting friends and family who encountered a similar misfortune yet connecting with individuals locally who are lamenting can be a huge advantage. Nobody ought to be let be to lament. Restorative to be with others are going through a similar close to home excursion and to discuss the effect of sorrow on one's life.

It might shock you how comparative your misery experience is to other people, and discussing it transparently can offer a degree of recuperating that is unmatched. Interfacing with others and having comparative sentiments is a restorative encounter that can assist with the lamenting system and work with mending.

Whether it's sharing stories or standing by listening to your cherished one's number one music, these little endeavors can have a major effect on some. Helping other people has the additional advantage of cheering you up as well.Remember and commend the existences of your friends and family. Commemorations of a lost cherished one can be a troublesome time for loved ones, however it can likewise be a period for recognition and respecting them. It is possible that you choose to gather gifts to a most loved foundation of the departed, giving a family name to a child or establishing a nursery in memory. What you pick is doing you, the length of it permits you to respect that extraordinary relationship such that feels right to you.

5. Keep a sound eating routine
A significant piece of taking care of oneself is eating great. During a time of sorrow, it might feel challenging to satisfactorily eat. Some of the time misery, tension and actual side effects of sorrow can bring about a demolished eating routine and diminished capacity to ordinarily eat. Due to these physical and profound requests, consuming a solid diet is much more essential.

Eating a good arrangement of nutrients and minerals is a significant piece of overseeing melancholy and burdensome side effects. Staying away from void starches, sweet food varieties and liquor are likewise significant elements in keeping a solid eating regimen during times of melancholy. Regardless of whether you end up eating modest quantities all at once over the course of the day, making the most of those food decisions can have a significant effect in how your body feels and recuperates.

Recollect that rolling out intense dietary improvements during a time of pain may not be the smartest thought. Maybe you can keep up with your standard eating designs during this time, and integrate quality food varieties for sadness. Extraordinary changes during seasons of anguish can be dangerous. It could be ideal to roll out little improvements, and this incorporates your dietary propensities.

6. Get rolling

Utilizing activity to adapt to pain is a sound methodology for mending. Exercise and sorrow are a decent blend as a result of the regular lift that exercise offers your brain and body. In addition to the fact that exercise works on cardiovascular wellbeing, yet it likewise delivers endorphins in the mind that make sensations of prosperity. Practice helps despondency in numerous ways, and distress is no special case.

Whether you take up trekking, running, yoga or basically strolling with a companion, there is no incorrect method for getting it done. Integrating exercise into your everyday schedule can essentially help your downturn and anguish insight. It very well might be useful to join an activity class where you can meet others and spotlight on a typical action. The interruption of meeting others in a social circumstance while partaking in some sound active work is an extraordinary way of dealing with stress for distress and sorrow.

The demonstration of getting more on top of your body's requirements and reinforcing your actual wellbeing is an optimal method for treating yourself well during your season of sadness. Exercise won't fix melancholy, yet it is a sound technique for managing troublesome feelings when they emerge.

7. Comprehend that pain is unusual
Sadness can cause you to feel all the way wild, which is a startling inclination and can bring a lot of inconvenience. The unconventionality of the lamenting system is ordinary. You might observe that you are crying at startling times. Overwhelming inclinations can arise,

apparently from no place, and can seize any given second during times of pain.

It could be that during your sadness cycle, you end up giving up to the tides of feeling really go. It might appear like you are helpless before these overwhelming inclinations, and that is totally typical. The more you attempt to stay away from sentiments and keep up with control, the more troublesome it will be to recuperate from distress.

Keep in mind, nobody ought to anticipate that you should be "finished" it, or to "snap out" of anguish. There is no particular time span for sadness, and it is individual and special to the individual encountering it. Your sentiments might be flighty, and that will be normal during a period of extraordinary misfortune.

8. Show restraint toward yourself
As you experience the scope of feelings that accompany pain, show restraint toward yourself. You might have times in which you keep thinking about whether you will at any point feel fine in the future. Sit with those

minutes and trust yourself to mend. It will work out, and it requires investment. Be delicate with yourself.

Pay attention to what your psyche, body and soul are requesting and honor your requirements similarly as you would respect the necessities of your cherished one who has passed. Frequently we hold ourselves to an unexpected norm in comparison to we do others. Ask yourself how you would treat a companion who was lamenting and give yourself a similar sort of sympathy and love.

Lamenting takes time. There is no alternate way around it. It is a characteristic interaction we experience when we care profoundly for somebody who has passed on. Offer yourself the adoration, generosity, empathy and persistence that you would provide for a companion.

9. Search out help
Looking for help is urgent during seasons of sadness. Backing can emerge out of companions, family, sorrow support gatherings,

distress guides and online help choices. Local area asset guides and nearby postings are many times the best places to find support gatherings. Many doctor's workplaces have arrangements of help assets accessible locally. Most nearby emergency clinics have associations with social laborers and hospice programs. These assets generally offer anguish support gatherings to individuals, everything being equal.

There are innumerable ways of getting to help, and the significant step is to connect and request it. Once in a while when distress is overpowering, it very well may be challenging to request help, yet recall that individuals aren't telepaths. The most effective way you can find support and backing is to tell others you are battling. Anguish doesn't need to be compounded by forlornness. Support is accessible and available in the event that you can venture out of connecting.

10. Acknowledge your new situation
One of the last phases of sadness is acknowledgment. Right off the bat in the

lamenting system, it might feel unimaginable that you might at any point come to a position of acknowledgment of this new reality without your cherished one. Tolerating sorrow and misfortune is a well deserved achievement in the lamenting system. There are phases of distress, and it is ordinary to go through these fluctuating stages at various times during your mending cycle and even re-visitation of earlier stages right when you think you've wrapped up with them.

As you explore this new reality that incorporates misfortune and distress, you may ultimately foster a feeling of significance around your misfortune, or an acknowledgment that this despondency experience has transformed you in significant ways. Melancholy can be a gift, and it can wake you up to the significant parts of life and take you back to your guiding principle through this serious torment and misfortune.

As you embrace your new situation, sadness can appear in changed ways that vibe more like a gift than you might have envisioned. Show restraint toward your development, your feelings and your recuperating cycle. A piece of embracing your new situation will lay out acknowledgment of development in the meantime. It is normal to encounter sensations of culpability while mending starts. Recall that your recuperating is important for the endowment of despondency and it respects your cherished one. It's anything but a double-crossing to recover and recuperate from misery; it is a characteristic, solid piece of the cycle.

Losing a friend or family member can be quite possibly of the most troublesome experience individuals face throughout everyday life. Adapting to sadness can appear to be a troublesome errand on occasion, and defeating pain can appear to be unthinkable. As you face misery, a significant variable is the assumption for recuperating. Rather than zeroing in on the most proficient method to conquer distress, a superior methodology is thinking about how to integrate this lamenting experience into your biography.

Notes